Dik-Dik

by Marilyn Brigham

Consultant: Darin Collins, DVM
Director, Animal Health Programs
Woodland Park Zoo
Seattle, Washington

BEARPORT PUBLISHING

New York, New York

Credits

Cover, © MyImages-Micha/Shutterstock; 3, © Volga2012/iStock; 4–5, © Oks88/Thinkstock; 6L, © Africa Studio/Shutterstock; 6–7, © JohnCarnemolla/Thinkstock; 8T, © Roy Coetzee/Shutterstock; 8B, © dangdumrong/Shutterstock; 9, © T.J. RICH/Nature Picture Library; 10–11, © Malcolm Schuyl/Minden; 11R, © Richard Garvey-Williams/nature/Ardea; 12L, © Maggy Meyer/Shutterstock; 12–13, © AfriPics.com/Alamy; 14–15, © Tui De Roy/Minden; 16, © Simon Hosking/Minden; 17, © Malcolm Schuyl/Minden; 18–19, © MyImages-Micha/Shutterstock; 20, © dpa picture alliance/Alamy; 21, © Peter Blackwell/Nature Picture Library; 22 (T to B), © anmbph/Shutterstock, © John Carnemolla/Shutterstock, and © Joel Sartore, National Geographic Photo Ark/National Geographic Creative; 23TL, © JohnCarnemolla/iStock; 23TR, © PhotocechCZ/Shutterstock; 23BL, © Jeff Thrower/Shutterstock; 23BR, © Rich Carey/Shutterstock.

Publisher: Kenn Goin
Senior Editor: Joyce Tavolacci
Creative Director: Spencer Brinker
Design: Debrah Kaiser

Library of Congress Cataloging-in-Publication Data

Names: Brigham, Marilyn, author.
Title: Dik-dik / by Marilyn Brigham.
Description: New York, New York : Bearport Publishing, [2018] | Series: Even weirder and cuter | Includes bibliographical references and index.
Identifiers: LCCN 2017034362 (print) | LCCN 2017042902 (ebook) | ISBN 9781684025244 (ebook) | ISBN 9781684024667 (library)
Subjects: LCSH: Dik-diks—Juvenile literature. | Antelopes—Juvenile literature.
Classification: LCC QL737.U53 (ebook) | LCC QL737.U53 B7427 2018 (print) | DDC 599.64/6—dc23
LC record available at https://lccn.loc.gov/2017034362

For more information, write to Bearport Publishing Company, Inc., 45 West 21st Street, Suite 3B, New York, New York 10010. Printed in the United States of America.

10 9 8 7 6 5 4 3 2 1

Contents

What's this weird
but cute animal?

It's a
dik-dik.

GIANT eyes!

Long, bendy snout!

5

A dik-dik is a tiny antelope.

It's only about the size of a small dog!

Dik-diks live on grassy plains in Africa.

Being small is dangerous.

Lions, hyenas, and crocodiles all hunt dik-diks.

When these antelope spot danger, they whistle through their snouts!

hyena

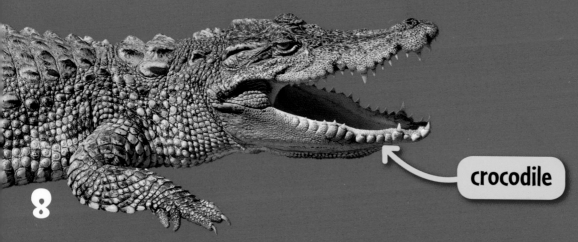

crocodile

8

Is that a
tiny trunk?

The dik-dik has a long, bendy snout.

It breathes and **pants** through its snout.

Panting helps keep the antelope cool in the hot sun.

Dik-diks rest in the shade during the hottest parts of the day.

Dik-diks are super fast!

They can run up to 26 miles (42 km) per hour.

That's about as fast as a horse!

Dik-diks are no match for lions, though. These big cats can sprint up to 50 miles (80 km) per hour.

13

Male and female dik-diks often live in pairs.

First, the male has to attract a **mate**.

To do this, he stands on his hind legs.

Then he waves to a female with his front legs.

Each dik-dik pair has its own **territory**.

They mark it with poop and stinky fluid.

a dik-dik pooping

The smells tell other animals to "Stay away!"

The stinky fluid comes from **glands**. These are found under the animals' eyes and between their toes.

Thirsty? Dik-diks rarely drink water.

They get most of the water they need from the plants they eat.

To break down the plants, dik-diks chew their food over and over again!

These small
antelope eat buds,
leaves, and grasses.

19

Twice a year, dik-dik pairs have one baby.

At birth, the baby is very small.

It can fit in an adult human's hand!

13-day-old dik-dik

Young dik-diks begin living on their own at just seven months old!

More Odd Antelope

Eland
This antelope from Africa is the world's largest. It weighs up to 2,000 pounds (907 kg). That's as heavy as a car!

Klipspringer
This little African antelope's name means "rock jumper." It can jump onto and balance on a rock as small as a silver dollar.

Royal Antelope
This West African animal is the tiniest antelope in the world. It's about the size of a large rabbit!

Glossary

glands (GLANDZ) body parts that produce chemicals

mate (MEYT) one of a pair of animals that have young together

pants (PANTZ) breathes hard and quickly to cool down

territory (TER-uh-tor-ee) an area of land that belongs to and is defended by an animal

Index

Read More

Gates, Margo. *Antelopes (Animal Safari).* Hopkins, MN: Bellwether Media (2013).

Gibbs, Maddie. *Antelope (Safari Animals).* New York: PowerKids Press (2011).

Learn More Online

To learn more about dik-diks, visit
www.bearportpublishing.com/EvenWeirderAndCuter

About the Author

Marilyn Brigham is a writer and editor living in New York City. She shares her home with her husband, baby, and a dog that's about the size of a dik-dik.